Becoming a Big Brother

Me, You, and Baby Ali
A Heartfelt Journey into Siblinghood

By: Louiza Amouri

Author of heartfelt stories for growing families

Becoming a Big Brother
Written & Illustrated by Louiza Amouri

Copyright © 2025 by Louiza Amouri
All rights reserved.

No part of this book may be reproduced, stored in a retrieval system, or transmitted in any form or by any means—electronic, mechanical, photocopying, recording, or otherwise—without the prior written permission of the copyright owner, except in the case of brief quotations used in reviews or articles.

Published by Louiza Amouri

ISBN: 979-8-9876777-8-0

Printed in the United States of America

For information, contact:
support@amouriprints.com

To Ryan, Zach, and Ali—
may your wild, caring, and joyful spirits
always make brotherhood your best adventure.

Hi, I'm Ryan. I'm the big brother.
That means I run faster, jump higher,
and tell the best knock-knock jokes in the
whole house

I thought,
awesome.
A sidekick!

Someone to play basketball with,
build pillow forts, and maybe
do my chores.

But Zach shook his head.

'Babies just cry...
...and stink...
and drool."
Yikes.

Zach and I started to wonder.
" When will he get here-tomorrow?"
"Do babies come by mail?"
Zach asked, squinting like he was waiting
for a package.

The waiting felt endless.
To pass time, we helped build the crib.

When mommy stepped away, Zach whispered in my ear: "I'll teach him how to climb out of it... hehe."

Zach pinched his nose.

I wasn't sure if babies were actually fun at all.

Sometimes, I felt a little...jealous.
Ali got so much attention. Everyone wanted
to hold him, take pictures of him,
even pinch his cheeks and give him lots of
hugs.

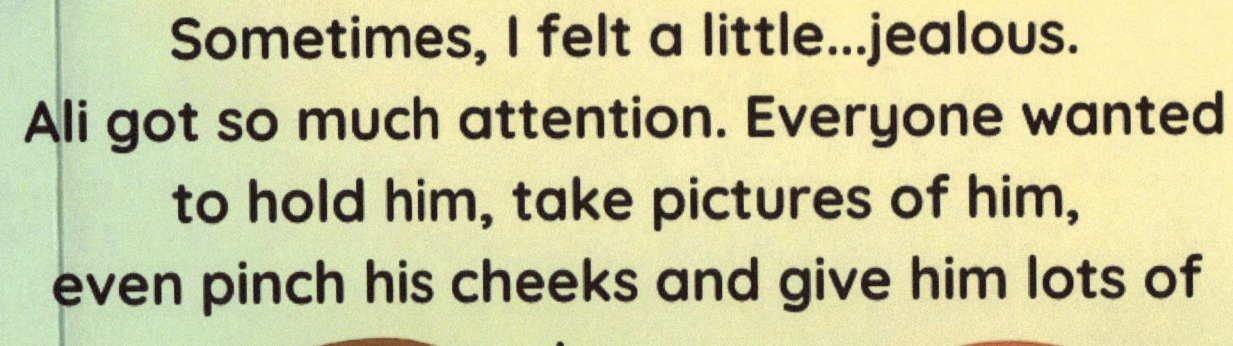

We imagined life with a new baby would be a hoot. But...Ali cried a lot!

I even asked my mom if he came with an off switch.

He just wiggles, drools, and makes the loudest fart noises.
(Okay, I admit... those are kind of funny.)

Zach peeked into the crib, and little Ali latched onto his finger with a huge smile that could melt the iciest heart!

So Zach and I made a plan:
We'll teach Ali soccer kicks,
videogames,
and how to sneak cockies when
Mom's not looking.
Because that's what
brothers are for.

One day Ali might run faster,
jump higher,
and sneak the last cookie.
But no matter what...
it's me, you, and baby Ali.
Forever the greatest team.

Louiza Amouri is a biomedical engineer turned children's book author. Storytelling has been her passion since childhood, beginning with tales she created for her little sister. Now, as a mom of three boys, she writes heartwarming stories that help families navigate big changes with love, laughter, and empathy.

When she's not writing or illustrating, Louiza can be found reading with her kids, sketching new characters, or dreaming up her next adventure in family storytelling.

She hopes this book brings comfort and joy to families welcoming a new baby.

www.ingramcontent.com/pod-product-compliance
Lightning Source LLC
Chambersburg PA
CBHW040028050426
42453CB00002B/50